D0753614

READY, SET, DRAW!

ANIMALS

AILIN CHAMBERS

 Gareth Stevens
PUBLISHING

Please visit our website, **www.garethstevens.com**. For a free color catalog of all our high-quality books, call toll free 1-800-542-2595 or fax 1-877-542-2596.

Library of Congress Cataloging-in-Publication Data

Chambers, Ailin.
Animals / by Ailin Chambers.
p. cm. — (Ready, set, draw!)
Includes index.
ISBN 978-1-4824-0908-6 (pbk.)
ISBN 978-1-4824-0909-3 (6-pack)
ISBN 978-1-4824-0907-9 (library binding)
1. Animals in art — Juvenile literature. 2. Drawing — Technique — Juvenile literature. I. Chambers, Ailin. II. Title.
NC780.C43 2015
743.6—d23

First Edition

Published in 2015 by
Gareth Stevens Publishing
111 East 14th Street, Suite 349
New York, NY 10003

Copyright © Arcturus Holdings Limited

Editors: Samantha Hilton, Kate Overy and Joe Harris
Illustrations: Dynamo Limited
Design concept: Keith Williams
Design: Dynamo Limited and Notion Design
Cover design: Ian Winton

All rights reserved. No part of this book may be reproduced in any form without permission from the publisher, except by reviewer.

Printed in the United States of America

CPSIA compliance information: Batch #CS15GS: For further information contact Gareth Stevens, New York, New York at 1-800-542-2595.

CONTENTS

GRAB THESE!

Are you ready to create some amazing pictures? Wait a minute! Before you begin drawing, you will need a few important pieces of equipment.

PENCILS

You can use a variety of drawing tools, such as pens, chalks, pencils, and paints. But to begin use an ordinary pencil.

PAPER

Use a clean sheet of paper for your final drawings. Scrap paper is useful and cheap for your practice work.

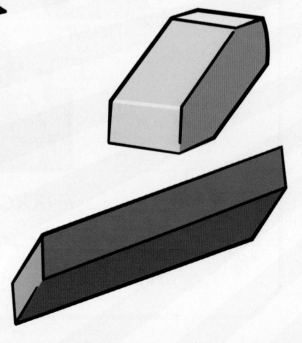

ERASERS

Everyone makes mistakes! That's why every artist has a good eraser. When you erase a mistake, do it gently. Erasing too hard will ruin your drawing and possibly even rip it.

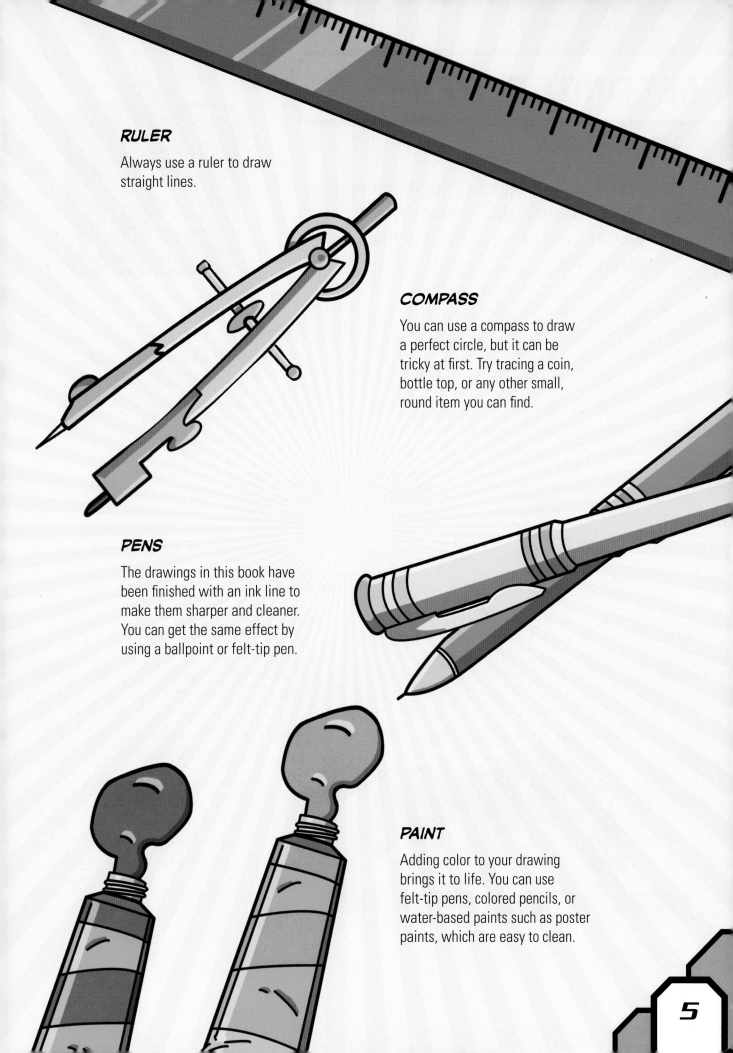

RULER

Always use a ruler to draw straight lines.

COMPASS

You can use a compass to draw a perfect circle, but it can be tricky at first. Try tracing a coin, bottle top, or any other small, round item you can find.

PENS

The drawings in this book have been finished with an ink line to make them sharper and cleaner. You can get the same effect by using a ballpoint or felt-tip pen.

PAINT

Adding color to your drawing brings it to life. You can use felt-tip pens, colored pencils, or water-based paints such as poster paints, which are easy to clean.

GETTING STARTED

In this book, we use a simple two-color system to show you how to draw a picture. Just remember: New lines are blue lines!

STARTING WITH STEP 1

The first lines you will draw are very simple shapes. They will be shown in blue. You should draw them with a normal pencil.

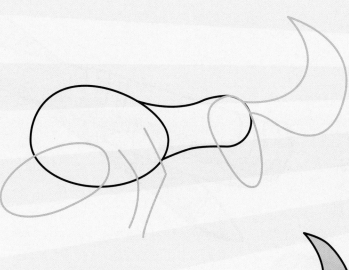

ADDING MORE DETAIL

As you move on to the next step, the lines you have already drawn will be shown in black. The new lines for that step will appear in blue.

FINISHING YOUR PICTURE

When you reach the final stage you will see the image in full color with a black ink line. Inking a picture means tracing the main lines with a black pen. After the ink dries, use your eraser to remove all the pencil lines before adding your color.

HAPPY

Draw wide-open eyes and raised eyebrows to create a happy face.

EMOTIONS

Once you've learned how to draw the animals in this book, you might want to try drawing them with different expressions. They could look happy, sad, angry, or even puzzled.

ANGRY

Add straight lines for eyebrows, an open mouth, and a jagged line for teeth. Now, he looks angry!

SURPRISED

Big eyes and one raised eyebrow, together with a round mouth, make your bear look surprised.

SAD

By curving the bear's eyebrows and mouth down, you can make him look sad.

THINKING

A pointed eyebrow and a slightly curved mouth make him look as if he's thinking about something.

EYES

As you can see, it's very easy to change expressions. You can completely alter your character by just changing the eyes and eyebrows.

Here are a few eyes to try drawing. From the top, these eyes are: surprised, sleepy, scared, angry, and sneaky.

GORILLA

A gorilla has a large head, and its arms are longer than its legs. It often walks on all fours.

STEP 1

First, draw a simple shape that looks like a Ping-Pong paddle.

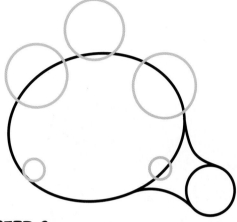

STEP 2

Next, add five circles to form the base for the gorilla's shoulders and elbows.

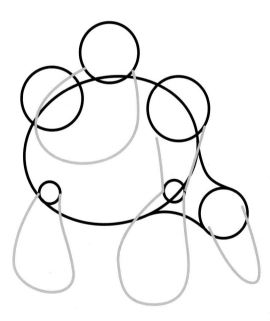

STEP 3

Now, add five more shapes to make its powerful arms, leg, and large jaw.

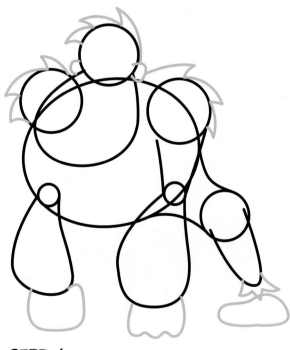

STEP 4

Draw small spikes to create the hair on the gorilla's head and shoulders. Don't forget to draw its hands and feet.

STEP 5

Add more fur to the arms. Draw simple lines for your gorilla's face, lip, chest, toes, and back leg.

STEP 6

Color in your gorilla using two shades of the same color. You could use blue, gray, or brown.

PONY

A pony has short legs, a stocky body, and a long mane and tail. Follow these step-by-step instructions to draw your very own pony.

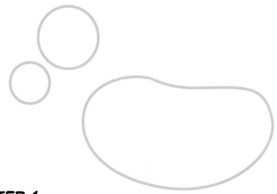

STEP 1

Start with two circles and a jelly bean shape to make the pony's head and body.

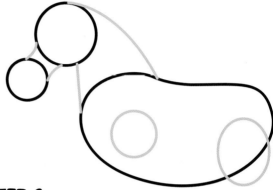

STEP 2

Link the three shapes together, and add a circle and an oval shape for the tops of the pony's legs.

STEP 3

Next, add six small circles for the leg and hoof joints. Draw an ear and the top of the pony's mane.

STEP 4

Draw lines to link the leg and hoof joints to create the pony's legs. Add nostrils, an eyelid, and the front part of the mane.

STEP 5

Draw its long, bushy mane and tail. Add hooves, complete its eye and eyebrow, and add its other ear.

STEP 6

You can color your pony any shade you like. Dapples, or the spots shown here, are a nice touch.

PANDA

A panda is a large black and white bear with a thick, woolly coat. It lives in the forests of China and spends most of its time eating bamboo.

STEP 1

Draw a large oval shape, slightly narrower at the top, to make your panda's body.

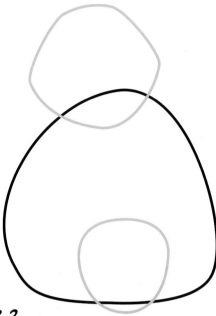

STEP 2

Add one oval to make the panda's head and another for its leg.

STEP 3

Next, add curved lines to make the panda's arms, ears, and outstretched leg.

STEP 4

Draw the panda's feet. Add large circles on its face to make its eye patches. Make a small nose.

A stick of bamboo is very simple to draw.

- Draw a rectangle like this.

- Draw in the lines for the bamboo segments.

- When you ink the picture, add curves between the lines. This will make the bamboo look bumpy.

STEP 5

Add a smiling face, eyebrows, eyes, claws and a panda's favorite food—a stick of bamboo.

STEP 6

Real pandas are black and white, but who says yours has to be? Why not try some other colors, such as purple and pink, or green and orange?

SHARK

A shark is a big fish with a smooth, streamlined body and powerful fins that help it glide swiftly through the water.

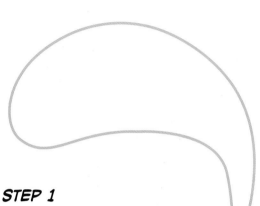

STEP 1

Draw a large teardrop shape to make the shark's sleek body.

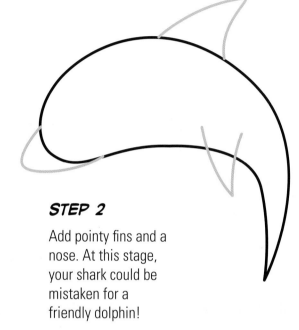

STEP 2

Add pointy fins and a nose. At this stage, your shark could be mistaken for a friendly dolphin!

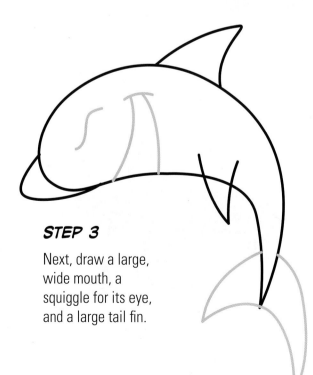

STEP 3

Next, draw a large, wide mouth, a squiggle for its eye, and a large tail fin.

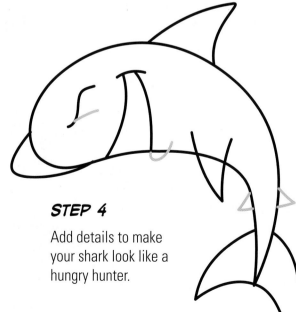

STEP 4

Add details to make your shark look like a hungry hunter.

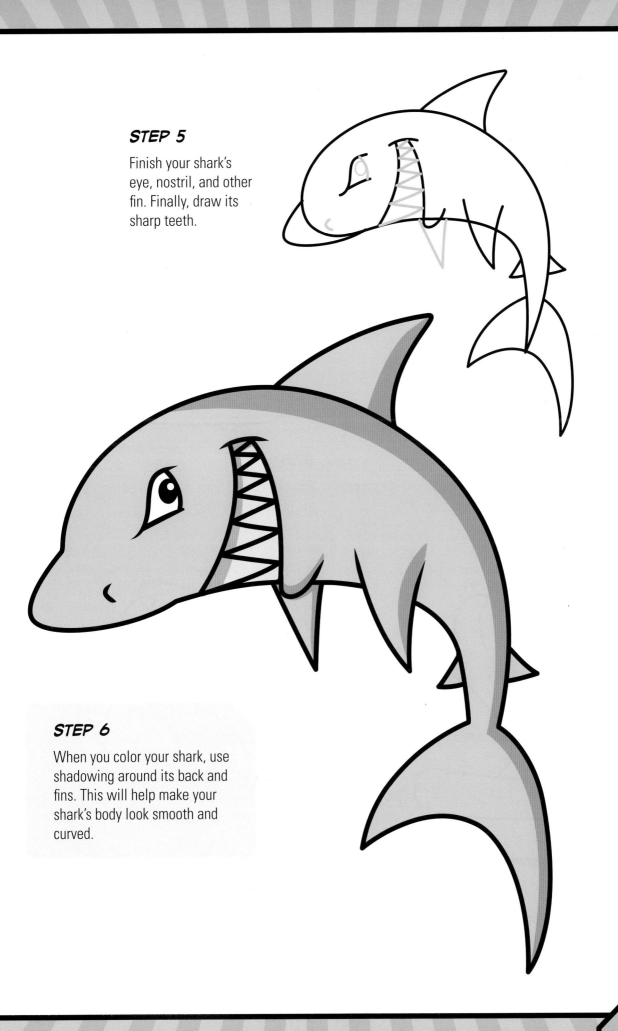

STEP 5

Finish your shark's eye, nostril, and other fin. Finally, draw its sharp teeth.

STEP 6

When you color your shark, use shadowing around its back and fins. This will help make your shark's body look smooth and curved.

RATTLESNAKE

A rattlesnake is a large snake with a rattle at the end of its tail. When it's surprised or about to attack, it coils its long body, rears up its head, and shakes its rattle loudly!

STEP 1

First, draw two long shapes that look like sausages to make the coils of your rattlesnake's body.

STEP 2

Add two curved lines that meet at the top to make the rattlesnake's long neck.

STEP 3

For the rattlesnake's head, draw a wide oval. Then add a long, pointy tail.

STEP 4

Next, add two eyebrow shapes on its head. Draw a line down one side of its neck and a small circle to create an extra coil.

STEP 5

Complete its face, and add a long, forked tongue. Draw V-shaped markings. You can color these in a different shade.

SUPER TIP!

A simple way to draw the snake's famous rattle is to build it from sausage shapes (just like its body).

Add sausage shapes to the tail, making each one smaller as you get closer to the tip.

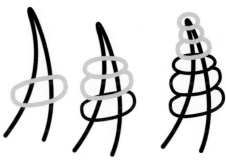

STEP 6

Draw a vertical line inside the eyeball. Then, add some colors.

GRIZZLY BEAR

A grizzly is a huge bear with thick, brown fur and a slightly flattened face. It has large, powerful paws and very long, sharp claws!

STEP 1

First, draw a squashed egg shape to make your bear's body.

STEP 2

Add the bear's feet. Then, draw a diamond shape for its head.

STEP 3

Now, it's time to start building the bear's body. Add arms, legs, ears, and a nose with these simple shapes.

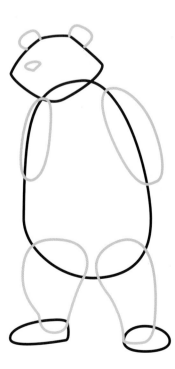

STEP 4

Finish the bear's arms with two more shapes. Then, add a long brow and muzzle.

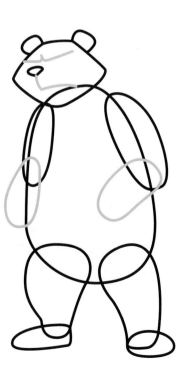

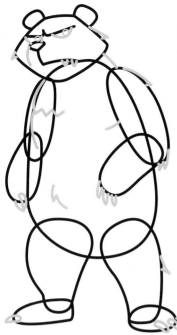

STEP 5

Next, add your bear's eyes, sharp claws, and teeth.

STEP 6

Finally, don't forget its thick, brown fur.

SUPER TIP!

To make drawing fur on animals simple, follow the rule of "less is more." You will save yourself a lot of time by not overcrowding your drawing with too much detail.

- Draw the line of the body smoothly.

- Use jagged lines in some parts of the outline to hint at the body being covered in fur.

- To give a large area a furry texture, you only have to draw a few small zigzag-shaped fur marks, rather than covering the whole body.

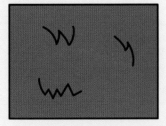

TIGER

A tiger is the largest of the big cats. Its striped body helps it to blend perfectly into its jungle surroundings.

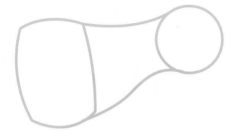

STEP 1

Start by drawing a rectangle and a circle. Link them together with two curved lines.

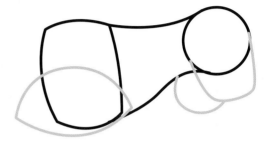

STEP 2

Add these three shapes to create the main part of the tiger's head and its back legs.

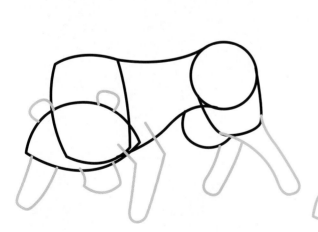

STEP 3

Add a pair of ears to the top of its head, and draw the rest of its legs. The small shape at the bottom of the tiger's head will be its lower jaw.

STEP 4

Next, draw the eyes, nose, muzzle, feet, and tail. Make sure you draw its tail using curved lines with no sharp angles.

SUPER TIP!

Start the tiger's stripes with simple, single lines. You can use straight lines, curved lines, or zigzags. Then, draw lines on either side of that first line to make the shapes shown here.

STEP 5

Add eyelids and eyes to complete the tiger's face. If you want your tiger to look nicer, draw the eyelids higher up its face. Draw simple lines for its stripes.

STEP 6

Color your tiger bright orange and black.

KITTEN

A kitten is a young cat with soft fur, a large head, big eyes and ears, and a long tail. Kittens are playful and are popular pets.

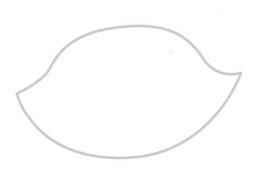

STEP 1

First, draw a shape a bit like a lemon. A kitten's head is big compared to the rest of its body.

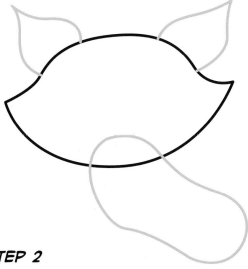

STEP 2

Add two large ears on top and a fat sausage shape for your kitten's body.

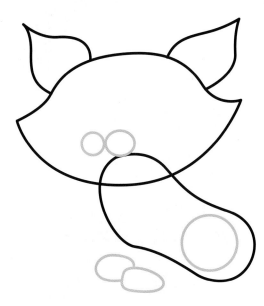

STEP 3

Next, add a large circle for the back leg, two small circles for the face, and two ovals for the front paws.

STEP 4

Draw two large eyes. Then, add a little nose, and complete the back leg and front legs.

STEP 5

Now, fill in the final details. Add eyes, eyebrows, a small mouth, fur around the ears and cheeks, and a long tail.

SUPER TIP!

Your kitten doesn't have to be the same color as this one. As you can see, a simple color change gives your furry friend a completely different look.

Why not color a few of them differently and have a whole litter of cuddly, fluffy kittens?

STEP 6

Your kitten can be any color. Adding small white spots in its eyes will create a cute, shiny effect.

23

PUPPY

A puppy is a young dog. When it's happy or excited, a puppy wags its tail from side to side.

STEP 1

Start by drawing a simple circle. You could trace around a coin to make your circle.

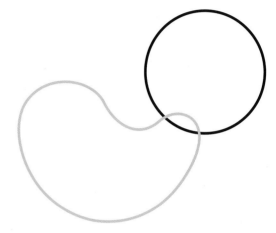

STEP 2

Then, add a shape that looks like a big jelly bean to make the puppy's body.

STEP 3

Four more circular shapes will make its muzzle and feet.

STEP 4

Draw curved front legs to make it look as if your puppy is about to jump up. Add a back leg. Draw big, floppy ears and a large nose on its muzzle.

STEP 5

Next, draw its big eyes, and draw its mouth and tongue. Then, complete the paws and other back leg. Finally, don't forget its tail!

STEP 6

You can choose any pattern you like to color your puppy's body. You could try some large patches or small spots, such as the ones you see on Dalmatians.

PARROT

A parrot is a bird with brightly colored feathers, a large, curved beak, and claws.

STEP 1

First, draw a pear shape to make the parrot's body.

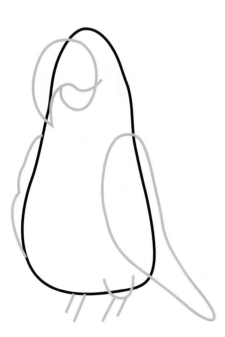

STEP 2

Next, add simple wing shapes and a large, hooked beak.

STEP 3

Add long, curved claws and a large eye. Then, draw some plumage on top of your parrot's head.

SUPER TIP!

You don't have to draw every feather on a parrot's body. If you want to make it look like it has feathers all over, just draw some little patches of feather shapes. They should be spaced out over its body and wings.

STEP 4

Add the branch and more detail on the eye.

STEP 5

Give the parrot some long tail feathers. Then, add more feathers on the body.

Now, you can color
your parrot using
bright colors.

A wolf is a wild animal with a large head, long legs, big paws, and a thick, furry coat. Wolves hunt other animals, and they have strong jaws and sharp teeth.

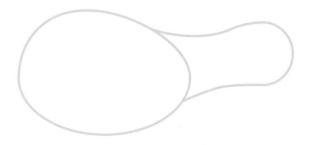

STEP 1

First, draw a large egg shape to make the wolf's hunched shoulders. Then, add a longer shape to make its body.

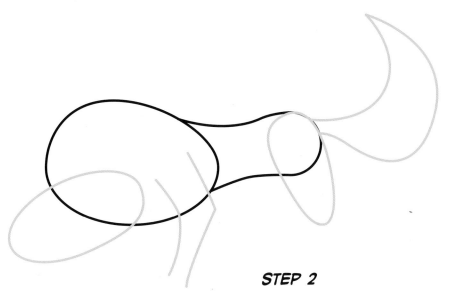

STEP 2

Draw another smaller oval to make the wolf's head. Then, add the top of its front leg, the top of its back leg, and a thick tail.

STEP 3

Add ears, a lower jaw, and paws to the front leg. Then, follow the lines for the back legs, as shown here.

STEP 4

Add a muzzle and nose to the wolf's face. Draw another front paw, back paw, and some of its fur.

STEP 5

Complete the wolf's eyes, add the last paw, and draw more fur.

STEP 6

Gray colors will give your wolf a scary look. A brightly colored wolf wouldn't last very long in the wild!

GLOSSARY

bamboo A kind of giant grass, with lots of tough, hollow stems.

Dalmatian A type of large dog with black spots and patches on a white coat.

dapples Rounded patches of different colors on an animal's coat.

muzzle The nose and mouth of an animal, such as a horse or dog.

plumage The feathers of a bird.

stocky Broad and sturdy.

vertical Up and down (rather than across).

FURTHER READING

Draw 50 Animals by Lee J. Ames (Watson-Guptill, 2012)

How to Draw Animals: A Step-by-Step Guide to Animal Art by Peter Gray (Arcturus Publishing, 2013)

WEBSITES

www.activityvillage.co.uk/learn-to-draw-animals

www.howtodrawanimals.net

www.wedrawanimals.com

INDEX